SO THAT'S HOW WE GOT THE BIBLE

SO THAT'S HOW WE GOT THE BIBLE

Bob Friedman
and Mal Couch

under the auspices of
The Evangelical Communications Research Foundation

TYNDALE HOUSE PUBLISHERS
Wheaton, Illinois

COVERDALE HOUSE PUBLISHERS LTD.
London, England

Artist: Ron Adair

So That's How We Got the Bible. Library of Congress Catalog Card Number 73-81013. ISBN 8423-6090-5. Copyright © 1973 by Tyndale House Publishers, Wheaton, Illinois. First printing, June 1973. Printed in the United States of America

Contents

1

Right On or Dead Wrong

A book tracing the history of the English Bible may sound as exciting as being sergeant-at-arms at a meeting of retired hot dog vendors. You know—the kind of book where nothing makes sense, the facts presented have no personal meaning for you, and there's not even enough room in the margins to doodle properly.

We hope to change that image by saying a few things which may have escaped your notice. If you're willing to spend a little time exploring that musty old black book called the Bible, we're willing to show you why the cover—and the contents—may be more colorful than you think.

O.K. Many people think the Bible was written by do-gooders hoping to take all the fun out of life. You can't do this, or that, or anything!

Yet the Bible itself says it is the Word of God, something which goes beyond morality. If the writers of the Bible were lying about this they couldn't be very moral persons, and you would have to throw out the "morality" tag along with the Book.

But if the Bible *is* in fact the Word of God it's time to find out what the Author has to say—in language we understand.

From the first page of Genesis in the Old Testament, to the last page of Revelation in the New Testament, God outlines a course of human history. It begins with man and moves to an eternity of dynamic joy reserved for those who have believed his Word. Thousands, perhaps millions, century after century, have claimed that God zapped them into a higher plane of awareness, a higher state of happiness, and a life with real purpose.

And to prove his continual love, and provide guidance for man, the Bible claims this God reached down and chose a king. Or shepherd. Or fisherman. Nearly forty different persons over a period of about 1,500 years wrote down what God had to say.

Another book on morals? Not likely. God was interested in much more than man's conduct.

The word "Bible" comes from the name of the papyrus or *byblus* reed used by the old-timers to make scrolls way back before the time of color televisions, even before radio! By the second century A.D. the Scriptures were referred to by the Greek Christians as *Ta Biblia,* "the books."

Through one more change into Latin and another into English it came out *Bible.* One book containing two testaments. Those who forget it's one book, attempting to separate the testaments, often get into real trouble. We won't do that.

Over the years one scientist after another has gotten his daily laughs by insisting certain historical references or claims in the Old Testament were not as factual as an average science fiction story.

The idea of one God, many claimed, grew from an army of gods made from sticks, stone, brass, and gold which were worshiped by our "heathen" ancestors. Yet the Scriptures, as a source of prehistory, tell the story in reverse. The Bible states man worshiped one God, *then* became lost in a tangled mess of anthropomorphic do-it-yourself kits. And every time an archeologist digs into the Mideast soil, something turns up that proves the Bible's point.

Archeological excavations have shown over and over again that the Hebrew record could easily have been written at the time it claims to be, although certain scholars assumed writing was an unknown practice in Palestine at the time Moses hiked to the Promised Land.

The earliest Hebrew document discovered to date is the Gezer Calendar, written about 925 B.C. as part of a schoolboy's exercise. This indicates writing was so widely used that children were normally taught this art.

The Ras Shamra Tablets, found in 1929, date from about 1400 B.C. Its 30-letter alphabet resembles Hebrew more than any other Semitic dialect.

Hieroglyphic inscriptions have been found dating from 1500 B.C. at the very latest. The authors of these writings were Semitic miners employed by Egypt, indicating writing was common enough for even the lower classes to use.

Then again, some historians have even attacked the Genesis account of good old Abraham, doubting such a man could have lived in such a place so long ago. Yet from 1922 to 1934 Leonard Woolley excavated the city of Ur, Abraham's home town, and discovered a large and advanced civilization at about 2000 B.C.— during Abraham's time. Reading, writing, arithmetic, and religion were taught.

An archeological dig

Genesis 13 has taken its knocks from those maintaining that the Jordan Valley was almost uninhabited in Abraham's time—a "fact" which would contradict Abraham's story. However, as you may have guessed, more than seventy sites have been uncovered in the Jordan Valley— some as old as 3000 B.C.

Need we go on? Of course not. See, you needn't bury your head in the sand out of frustration when seeking to back up the Bible historically. But in case you do, look around down there; you never know what you may find . . .

Big deal, right? Scientists have determined that the Bible could very easily have been written when scriptural accounts say they were written. We determine the age of an account by historically dating material from *within* the account.

So what? Suppose Moses *did* write those five books that lead the whole thing off. And Jeremiah threw in his two cents worth. And Isaiah. And Daniel.

The fact remains that if these Hebrew prophets were merely recording their personal impressions of city life, farming methods, or how ugly their neighbor's wife was, it wouldn't mean much. After all, everybody has opinions. But the Bible claims these men weren't just composing for the fun of it. Rather, God himself, working through his Spirit, moved upon these men in such a way that every word they wrote was inspired.

Oh, now wait a minute . . .

Every word? That's what it says (we'll get around to the specific verse a little later). As for now let's see what this concept of "inspiration" is all about.

Inspiration says you take a primary cause, or force, like God's Spirit. This Spirit picks out a man and in a loud, authoritative voice says, "Hey, you!" then proceeds to fill this person with a warm knowledge of God's revelation.

This revelation is then written down by the man and becomes, literally, the Word of God. Remember, God respects men as individuals. Therefore, literary styles vary depending on the author; but this doesn't make the Scripture any less the Word of God.

Now set the scene. It's a dusty, wind-blown day several hundred years ago when Jeremiah faces off with Hananiah. Each claims to be a prophet of God. Each claims to be "inspired."

Hananiah promises, in contrast to Jeremiah's earlier prophecy, that Babylon would free the Jews from their captivity within two years. Jeremiah later informs his opponent that God said Hananiah would die that very year for being a false prophet. Sure enough, he dies.

Which only goes to show that if you state you're a prophet of God you better be able to put your prophecies where your mouth is.

But there are better ways of proof . . .

"If there is a prophet among you," God says in Deuteronomy 13, "or one who claims to foretell the future by dreams, and if his predictions come true but he says, 'Come, let us worship the gods of other nations,' don't listen to him.

"For the Lord is testing you to find out whether or not you really love him with all your heart and soul. You must *never* worship any God but Jehovah; obey only his commands and cling to him.

"The prophet who tries to lead you astray must be executed . . ."

Uh, oh. Bad news. And to further emphasize his point:

"But any prophet who falsely claims that his message is from me, shall die. And any prophet who claims to give a message from other gods must die" (Deuteronomy 18:20).

The ancients would stone to death any "prophet" who was wrong just once. Sounds as if an insurance company would consider "prophet" a high-risk business!

Also, if a prophet practiced any type of divination, augury, sorcery and such, he was to be immediately rejected.

It was also characteristic of true prophets that they only spoke when they felt led by God's Spirit. A prophet couldn't solicit a message from God or prepare a short speech to help the Man out.

Often God would pick up after the late, late show was over, for he made it clear that "even with a prophet, I would communicate by visions and dreams" (Numbers 12:6).

Swing back to today for a second. Are you familiar with those big tent revivals which television and films so often make fun of? You know, where the preacher praises God for an hour, steps behind the curtain for a few slugs of whiskey, then pinches a couple of teen-age assistants before hitting the pulpit again.

Just as a few preachers may act like this today, it wasn't any different way back when. Skip around the Old Testament and you'll find a few false prophets who were mercenaries, who prophesied for hire, were drunks, profane and wicked, frauds, treacherous, committed adultery, and were generally all-around bad guys.

You may be a "pre-med" major with hopes of becoming a doctor, but there was no such thing as being a "pre-prophet" student. It made no difference what you knew, *who* you knew, or how much spiritual training you had received.

God alone picked his prophets and that's that.

"But Amos replied, 'I am not really one of the prophets. I do not come from a family of prophets. I am just a herdsman and fruit picker. But the Lord took me from caring for the flocks and told me, "Go and prophesy to my people Israel"'" (Amos 7:14, 15).

A simple shepherd becomes a prophet. It's funny how God has no class consciousness. He'll deal with anyone.

Because a test of a true prophet rested in his prophecies, he had to be right in his predictions. Yet even false prophets were often correct, or performed miracles, so by itself this was not conclusive.

The Hebrews made sure a prophet's words were not in conflict with the prophecies of established prophets. If they weren't in agreement, then out went the would-be prophet.

Stealing prophecies was also a big thing. How better to sound like a prophet than a little plagiarism on the side? You may not think this kind of verbal hanky-panky would get God uptight, but just listen:

"So I stand against these 'prophets' who get their messages from each other—these smooth-tongued prophets who say, 'This message is from God!' Their made-up dreams are flippant lies that lead my people into sin . . ." (Jeremiah 23:30-32).

God, using truth to lead his people toward himself, often led his prophets to declare things which proved to be most unpopular with the masses. With no concern for his own well-being, the true prophet became a messenger of God and a target of the people.

False prophets played it safe. They'd size up

the present situation and tell the folks all kinds of good news to appease their egocentric appetites. A false prophet was a good con-man, but when God let him have it . . . whap!

Another test of whether a man was a true prophet rested with the inner message of God's Spirit acting upon individuals. You know—good vibes or bad vibes.

After listening to a false prophet ramble on for a while the persons closest to God would have no trouble deciding the guy was a fake, by his actions, his words, and lack of spiritual charisma.

Besides the term "prophet," a man chosen by God was often called a man of the Spirit, a watchman, a seer or beholder, a man of God, a servant of the Lord, or a messenger of the Lord.

To sum it all up, a prophet was one who received a revelation from the Lord and let the people know about it. God's mouthpiece.

The Lord wasn't satisfied with a few displays of oral excellence, so he often commanded these prophets to stop shouting long enough to write down what he had shown them.

"Make a large signboard and write on it . . ." (Isaiah 8:1).

"And the Lord said to Moses, 'Write down these laws that I have given you . . .'" (Exodus 34:27).

"Get another scroll and write everything again

just as you did before" (Jeremiah 36:28).

And to illustrate how God fully intended his Word to last longer than the next day's newspaper, he told Isaiah:

"Now go and write down this word of mine concerning Egypt, so that it will stand until the end of time, forever and forever . . ." (Isaiah 30:8).

To ward off claims of cynics that the Scriptures were a hit-or-miss stew of God's meat in man's gravy, the Lord placed himself on the witness stand and wrote his defense.

He had this thing about letting people know that what he wrote through the prophets, *he wrote*! For example:

"These are the commandments and ordinances which the Lord gave to the people of Israel through Moses . . ." (Numbers 36:13).

"Joshua recorded the people's reply in the book of the laws of God . . ." (Joshua 24:26).

From one prophetical book to another we read phrases like:

"These are the messages that came to Isaiah . . . God showed him what was going to happen . . ." (Isaiah 1:1, 2).

"These are God's messages to Jeremiah . . ." (Jeremiah 1:1).

Twenty-six of the Old Testament's thirty-nine books have a direct claim that they are God's Word to man. Many books needn't state their own case since they're included in a section of books which do attest to their source.

Only the historical and poetic books may not have this type of direct statement, for they report what God *showed* to man rather than what he *said*. Yet all writings carry the same weight as being the Word of God.

Nehemiah, the last historical book in the Old Testament, states that the Lord most definitely spoke through his messengers:

"You were patient with them for many years. You sent your prophets to warn them about their sins, but they still wouldn't listen" (Nehemiah 9:30).

During hundreds of years, book after book was written. Some writings were inspired of God; others were perhaps historically correct but uninspired works of literature.

The religious leaders clearly had to decide which books were from the Boss and which ones weren't. After all, he'd want it that way. So try swallowing the following word:

Canonicity.

The ancient Greeks used the word *kanon* to signify a rod, ruler, staff, or measuring rod. This word is probably a derivative of the Hebrew *kaneh* (reed), which meant measuring rod.

The word canon, therefore, has come to mean a standard or norm. In about 350 A.D. Athanasius the Greek was the first person definitely known

13

to have applied the term canon to the Scriptures.

Over the ages different ideas have been proposed in an attempt to decide what was canonical, a true book of God, and what wasn't. For instance, some have said that the older the book the more right it had to be called a part of the canon. Yet this theory is blown to bits when you consider that many ancient books in Hebrew literature, books older than some canonical pieces, were not admitted to the Scriptures.

These books are referred to in the Bible itself: "The Book of the Wars of Jehovah," (Numbers 21:14); "The Book of Jashar," (Joshua 10:13); or "Detailed biographies of King David have been written in the history of Samuel the prophet, the history written by Nathan the prophet, and in the history written by the prophet Gad" (1 Chronicles 29:29).

Most of the Scriptures were judged canonical soon after they had been written. Moses was still alive when his writing was placed into the ark (Deuteronomy 31:24-26); Daniel accepted his older contemporary Jeremiah's book as canonical (Daniel 9:2); and Ezekiel referred to Daniel (Ezekiel 28:3).

Others have stated that a book was canonical if written in the Hebrew language. This simply isn't true, since the Hebrews rejected many books written in their own language. Also, books which have been accepted, such as Daniel

and Ezra, contain parts written in Aramaic—
so the Old Testament is not completely written
in Hebrew.

A book is canonical because it was inspired
by God. Period. When men *discovered* which
books these were they determined the writings
came with the authority of God and were prophetic. They were written by a true prophet and
the man's prophecies came true.

Books in the canon also told the truth about
God, they weren't inconsistent with his nature,
and they told the truth about man as God had
established.

Scriptures come with the *power* of God, they
back up their claims with action, and God-
breathed writings are accepted by God's people—
true believers. Books were not accepted if supported only by isolated religious cults.

Much of the Apocrypha, or noncanonical
writings, were tossed out by the early Jewish
and Christian scholars because they were second-
class items: full of historical inaccuracies and
moral no-nos.

Most scholars can agree that the Old Testament
finally got it all together by 100 B.C. The standard
or Masoretic text of the Hebrew Old Testament
contains 24 books, beginning with Genesis and
ending with 2 Chronicles. It is most commonly divided into three divisions: the Law (the first five
books of Moses), the Prophets, and the Writings.

The Protestant Bible contains the same divisions but arranges the twenty-four Hebrew volumes into thirty-nine books, separating several which were linked together by the Hebrews.

Many persons believe the Bible was written hundreds of years after the indicated events, although we hope we've presented sufficient evidence to the contrary. If all this isn't enough proof for you, then consider what happened in 1947 when an Arab shepherd boy started chasing a lost goat.

Little Muhammad adh-Dhib was searching for an animal a mile west of the Dead Sea and about seven miles south of Jericho. He explored a cave, found some large clay jars containing many leather scrolls, and that was the beginning of the discovery of what we now call the Dead Sea Scrolls.

All this from chasing a goat. The results show that the Scriptures *are* as old as they claim to be. Of course no *originals* have been discovered, but just consider . . .

Before this discovery the Hebrew text was based on three partial and one complete manuscript dating from about 1000 A.D. Now we have the complete book of Isaiah and thousands of fragments dating from at least 100 B.C.

Discovery of the Dead Sea Scrolls

And if you think there was hardly any difference between the earliest Isaiah text and its counterpart a thousand years later, you're right.

Scholars now have thousands of manuscripts of the Old and New Testaments to consider, including the Septuagint, the Old Testament translated into Greek between 250 and 140 B.C.

Hundreds of prophecies in the Old Testament point to the promised Messiah of Israel, and it's with the expectancy of the coming of this Messiah that the Old Testament canon accepted no writings after Malachi wrapped it up about four hundred years before Christ.

In the noncanonical writings between the Old and New Testament times it is stated that the people were waiting "until a prophet should arise" (1 Maccabees).

Josephus, the great Jewish historian who lived about the time of Christ, wrote: "After the latter prophets Haggai, Zechariah, and Malachi, the Holy Spirit departed from Israel."

So about four hundred years after the Old Testament hung out a "No Admittance" sign to future writers, another Jewish "prophet" turned Jerusalem and the Mideast upside-down.

Within a hundred years after Jeshua (or, in Greek, Jesus) was born, another testament had been written. It was based on who Jesus claimed to be (the promised Messiah, the Son of God), his words and his deeds.

18

Amazingly enough this Jesus said, "Don't misunderstand why I have come—it isn't to cancel the laws of Moses and the warnings of the prophets. No, I come to fulfill them, and to make them all come true" (Matthew 5:17).

He put his seal of approval on the Old Testament canon and stated that everything which had been accepted as inspired of God from Genesis to Malachi was genuine.

"The Scriptures" are referred to over and over again by New Testament writers, verifying the authenticity of the Old Testament. Jesus suggested to the people they "search the Scriptures" in order to find himself revealed.

Astonish yourself—research the number of Old Testament verses quoted in the New Testament, testifying to the fact you can't separate the two.

In the Old Testament God sets up the Law and promises a deliverer. In the New Testament Jesus fulfills this Law as the deliverer.

Let's dig into the writing of the New Testament. Let's find out how the Bible began to bump along a dark, twisting road for centuries until we discovered that—yes, folks—God *does* speak English!

2

God Speaks English

"The whole Bible," the New Testament says, "was given to us by inspiration from God and is useful to teach us what is true and to make us realize what is wrong in our lives; it straightens us out and helps us do what is right" (2 Timothy 3:16).

Wow! Who but the God who created everything and knows man's heart better than man himself could ever make such a statement? You'll notice he doesn't say, "Pick and choose what you want, man."

Rather, he says the entire Bible is God's Word. And this Word can do more to give us understanding of ourselves and others—this Word can do more to give us one happy day after another than all the books on psychoanalysis you can find in a university library.

To drive the point home, we read in 2 Peter 1:20, 21: "For no prophecy recorded in Scripture was ever thought up by the prophet himself. It was the Holy Spirit within these godly men who gave them true messages from God."

New Testament writers claimed the same inspiration as did the Old Testament prophets. In fact, that word "inspired" in the Timothy verse above is translated from the Greek *theopneustros,* which means "God-breathed." You can't get closer than that.

To move from the Old Testament to the New, check out the first two verses of the book of Hebrews:

"Long ago God spoke in many different ways to our fathers through the prophets [in visions, dreams, and even face to face], telling them little by little about his plans.

"But now in these days he has spoken to us through his Son to whom he has given everything, and through whom he made the world and everything there is."

For about twenty years after Christ lived on earth there was no written account or comment about his person. All of the Gospels and letters later accepted as canon were finally written by about 95 A.D.

During those days of early evangelism the apostles and preachers of the day would constantly refer to their only Scriptures, the Old Testament, to prove that prophecies about the Messiah Jesus had in fact come true.

Peter preached Christ, using the Old Testament; Stephen gave a quick historic review of the Old Testament in his great sermon to the Jewish leaders; Philip used one of the greatest chapters in the Old Testament, Isaiah 53, to tell an Ethiopian about Jesus.

It's upon this firm background of understanding the Old Testament that the New Testament writers were able to show how God's grace had finally manifested itself through Christ.

O.K. So early believers in Christ told of his ministry by word-of-mouth, repeating over and over again stories of Jesus until they became almost uniform in their content.

After a community had heard these verbal reports about Jesus they wanted an authoritative account written for them which would relate the facts of Jesus' life and give them practical application for daily living.

The Apostle Paul's letters and other epistles were written to meet this need.

As you might expect, the people became

pretty curious about the exact life of Christ himself. After all, if you've been through a dynamic change in your life, and all of a sudden you can see things through God's eyes, then you kind of want to know the Man responsible.

Therefore the synoptic Gospels and the Gospel of John were written. The book of Acts was written by Luke to give a history of the apostles in the early church and John's Revelation was written to let believers of all ages know how God planned to wrap up his business on earth.

Even as canonical books were being written, other works of literature appeared and competed for a spot in the list of God-inspired Scripture.

The Apostle John wrote, "Jesus' disciples saw him do many other miracles besides the ones told about in this book" (John 20:30). Then he added, "And I suppose that if all the other events in Jesus' life were written, the whole world could hardly contain the books!" (John 21:25).

This may sound like a giant game of eenie-meenie-minie-mo was called for, but not true. God inspired either eye-witnesses to Jesus and his ministry or else men tied directly to eye-witnesses in order to produce the New Testament.

Even though it took a while to arrive at a standard New Testament canon, the evidence is there to show the actual writers were aware a canon was being formed.

For example, the Apostle Paul, who apparently did more writing than any of the other apostles, instructed the early churches to read his letters to everyone and then pass them on.

These churches copied and thereby collected these letters, reading with authority the prophetic and practical messages they received. To show these letters were not meant merely for a particular group, but for the entire church, we have Colossians 4:16: "By the way," Paul wrote, "after you have read this letter will you pass it on to the church at Laodicea? And read the letter I wrote to them."

No such thing as running off a quick Xerox of the letter, but after a speedy scribe copied the message they dropped it in the mail. First class.

There must have been many, many more letters written than God intended to be included in the New Testament. That letter to the Laodicean Church, for instance, has evidently been lost— so its usefulness was over when it was read by the recipients and by the Colossians. Otherwise God would have seen to it that it was safely preserved.

In the same way he quotes the Old Testament, Paul quotes from the Gospel of Luke, thereby treating both as Scriptures. In still another way of displaying how canonical books were immediately quoted as being God's Word, Jude says to "remember what the apostles of our Lord Jesus Christ told you" (Jude 17).

To sum up the origin of New Testament canon, the first stories of Jesus were passed on by eye-witnesses, then written down, circulated, collected, and quoted as being part of the Scriptures.

The writers knew they weren't just making a good guess or scribbling down something that sounded right. With insight and awareness Paul wrote: ". . . we have even used the very words given us by the Holy Spirit, not words that we as men might choose. So we use the Holy Spirit's words to explain the Holy Spirit's facts" (1 Corinthians 2:13).

It's this same Holy Spirit who Jesus promised would guide and lead all believers into a truth about himself. He never said the Scriptures were a matter of interpretation. He never said, "Believe what you want to." But just in case you think individual interpretation of the Scriptures is something new—a product of our "enlightened" society—then read what Peter had to say about what was happening to Paul's letters:

"Some of his comments are not easy to understand, and there are people who are deliberately stupid, and always demand some unusual interpretation—they have twisted his letters around to mean something quite different from what he meant, just as they do the other parts of the

Scripture—and the result is disaster for them" (2 Peter 3:16). One of man's favorite pastimes for hundreds of years has been twisting what Jesus said in order to make ourselves feel more self-confident.

Yet how can we be sure, assuming we'll believe whatever the Scriptures say, that these are in fact the original words? How do we know we haven't been aced out by some smart-aleck scribe who couldn't resist switching a few things around?

Some have suggested every translation is inspired in the same sense as the original. Yet since some errors of copyists have obviously crept into the Scriptures you would have to approve biblical duplications with errors as inspired. This conflicts with the very definition of inspiration we have established.

We're left with the originals, and only the originals, being the completely inspired Word of God. And yes, friends, there are no originals for us to gaze at.

The development of the sensitive skill of textual criticism has perfected the task of forming copies which are almost duplicates of original documents. This has resulted in an amazingly accurate objective science rather than a series of subjective guesses.

Such scholars conduct a critical study of the original language, seeking mechanical errors common to scribes. As they pursue textual criticism, they normally prefer the more difficult reading of two versions of the same passage (since a copyist would tend to simplify, not complicate material); they prefer the earliest manuscript (less chance of error); and choose the version in harmony with other Scripture.

Now—before you start blaming God for messing things up so bad that we've got to sweat it out before arriving at his true Word, why not consider:

That perhaps he gets upset when his people worship objects instead of himself. As when the Israelites worshiped the bronze serpent that Moses held up in the wilderness. Maybe God knows our eyes might be taken off him if we had the original Scriptures—we might have more reverence for them than we have for him.

Look, you can throw this whole discussion of perfect or near-perfect Scriptures into a large pot of skepticism and nit-picking and still come out with a clear solution, simply because there is no doctrine recognized by true believers which is based solely on one itsy-bitsy word or even one little phrase found in a particular version of the Bible.

While only the original writings were absolutely inspired, the copies available to us today are faithful, accurate versions of the originals. And if you take all of the spellings and words which scholars aren't quite sure of in the New Testament, they'd barely fill up one printed page.

So God's love and message for man really isn't the hidden secret some people make it out to be. It's there for the reading.

The fact the Lord inspired certain writings should have been motive enough to gather and save what's been written. But, of course, there were human motives for gathering a uniform canon.

First, if books were from God, and prophetic, they were invaluable as to guidance and instruction for believers and as the source of truth for nonbelievers.

Also, many believers took seriously the Lord's command to hit every area on earth and lay the gospel on the natives. As early as the first half of the second century much of the Bible was translated into Syriac and Old Latin, but you couldn't translate a Bible which didn't have it all together.

The missionaries put pressure on the church fathers to come up with a uniform canon, one set of specified books, which from then on would be a complete testament.

Then a rather devious soul, Diocletian, went on a kick of burning things just a little after A.D. 300. He threw assorted objects into the fire: like Bibles, churches, and Christians.

This persecution forced believers to decide

29

which books were canonical, since it was easier to risk your life defending God's Word than man's musings.

Such books as the Shepherd of Hermas, I Clement, and the Didache were thrown in with the Scriptures and tossed about for several years at the same time the canon was being formed.

Yet the canonical books—before the New Testament was finally decided upon—were mentioned consistently.

Polycarp (c. A.D. 150) was a young friend and follower of the Apostle John. In his writings he quoted freely from Matthew, John, ten of Paul's epistles, 1 Peter and 1 and 2 John.

At about the same time, Justin Martyr considered all the Gospels as being the real thing from God and often referred to most of the other books in the Bible.

Later on old Polycarp himself had a disciple in Irenaeus (c. A.D. 170). He either quoted from or considered authentic twenty-three of the final twenty-seven books.

Clement of Alexandria (c. A.D. 200) matched Irenaeus almost book for book. Before the end of the second century there were individuals who recognized nearly every book in the New Testament as being canonical. Books not on their lists had already been approved by other authorities years before.

It should be mentioned that not everything

went smoothly during this time, as you may have guessed. Take a joker like Marcion. In A.D. 140 he gave to the world his gift of the first New Testament canon that we know of. There was only one small problem.

Marcion accepted only the Gospel of Luke and ten of Paul's epistles. He threw everything else out. The Scripture which he did retain was subsequently translated, distorted, twisted, and changed beyond recognition in order to corroborate his own beliefs.

Justin Martyr, Irenaeus, and others were nice to Marcion. They simply called him a heretic.

Athanasius of Alexandria (A.D. 298 to 373) is considered the first to declare canonical the twenty-seven books we have in our New Testament. The councils of Hippo (A.D. 393) and Carthage (A.D. 397) agreed with Athanasius and others and approved the present canon.

In the centuries to follow, the church leaders obviously ignored most of what Jesus said, horribly twisted his Word, and helped to lead the world into the darkness of ignorance.

Watch where you're stepping. We're about to enter grim, bloody years of torture. During the Middle Ages.

The Real Thing

You've seen how God stayed up late on several occasions in order to "breathe" his Word through man. It's now time to remind you that man, with typical lack of appreciation, proceeded to ignore most of what God had been saying.

The early, dynamic Christian church which witnessed the power and love of the Messiah faded over the centuries until human ego trips took control of man's spiritual training.

The Old and New Testaments were always

there—God was always there—but for the most part society blindly ignored what the Lord had written.

Most of the Scriptures were written in Hebrew (Old Testament) or Greek (New Testament). Between A.D. 383 and 405 the Scriptures were translated into Latin by Jerome. This Latin Bible, or Latin Vulgate, was *the* translation coveted by church leaders for about one thousand years.

Jerome began his work soon after Christianity became the official religion of the Roman Empire in A.D. 380. The Romans set up a type of political-religious hierarchy which lasted for centuries, and, in many ways, has never ended.

To understand this you must remember "religion" was not what Jesus was preaching to the people. Rather, he talked of a personal *relationship*. He never instructed man to go out and establish hundreds of other traditions which only served to create a barrier between man and God.

Although the apostles did recommend the church have elders, deacons, and other leaders, they never intended for believers (or seekers) to walk through three offices and past five secretaries in order to rap with a counselor.

It was through a Roman named Leo that the idea of papal supremacy first became firm. Initially he did not have the exclusive title of Pope, as this Latin name for father (papa) had also applied to bishops and priests.

34

When Christianity became the state religion the leaders reaped the benefits of power, and attacked any who would oppose their universal, or catholic beliefs.

Those not swinging along with the Catholic church were called heretics. Their books were burned, meetings broken up, property taken away and, very often, the more stubborn heretics were put to death.

Yet for very good reasons the common man couldn't point to a Scripture verse and tell the church leaders to cool it—he didn't have a Bible to refer to. Furthermore, he could not read, even if he had had ten Bibles. The message which was to be spread to the whole world was safely locked up, often literally chained to the pulpit.

In 529, just north of Naples, a monastery was founded by Benedict. The big things going on up on the mountain were poverty and chastity. The monks would pray, sleep, read, teach, or farm. Perhaps they didn't know Jesus said: "Therefore go and make disciples in all the nations . . ." (Matthew 28:19). It's kind of hard to communicate when you're isolated on a mountain. Not too much traffic.

In 596 Augustine and forty monks went to England to become missionaries. Augustine became the first Archbishop of Canterbury, and the English Church, with a Latin Bible held by only a few, began to flourish.

Churches sprang up and, amidst the daily politics, much good was accomplished. A growing bureaucracy provided relief to the poor, care of the sick, room and board for travelers, and trained numbers of clerks to read and write.

But man just couldn't let go of himself. Have you ever read about old Simon Magus, a magician spoken about in the New Testament? It seems this dude wanted to *buy* God's Holy Spirit from Peter. From this Simon the people got the name simony—the buying and selling of church offices. From one relative to another the church leaders sold offices, and with the office went control of vast sums of money.

Ah, well. So it went. Marrying, burying, and caring for parishioners each developed a price tag. May we quote the Lord again?

"Let everyone see that you are unselfish and considerate in all you do. Remember that the Lord is coming soon. Don't worry about anything; instead, pray about everything; tell God your needs and don't forget to thank him for his answers" (Philippians 4:5, 6).

With God it's a promise. With man it costs money.

Despite popes fighting with princes and cardinals clashing with peasants, the story of the Son of God still found its way into the hearts of the people.

Many who longed to grab on to the stories of

Jesus simply looked at the church decorations. Paintings and relief carvings related events from the Gospels.

Poems were also used to carry on the message of Christ. Bede, an educated monk of Jarrow, wrote an account of a man named Caedmon—a hired hand at a Yorkshire monastery.

It seems Caedmon, completely lacking any creative talent, received words and music to a song praising God as he dreamed one night. Upon waking, the laborer remembered everything and immediately threw down a hoe and picked up a quill pen.

Caedmon is credited with writing musical themes based on Genesis, Exodus, and Daniel.

Bede, the monk who wrote about Caedmon, had an unusual concern for his fellow countrymen who were not able to fly through the Latin as he was. He translated certain parts of the New Testament into their own English tongue, and was working on the Gospel of John when he died in 735.

The English king Alfred (871-901) wasn't as big a dummy as many rulers of the day who often needed a companion to read the street signs for them. Alfred the Great even had a yen for culture and actually had translated into English Bede's *Ecclesiastical History of the English Nation*, Orosius's *Universal History*, and Pope Gregory the Great's *Pastoral Care*.

Years later the Wessex Gospels, an Old English translation, made the round of the scholars and later, near the end of the tenth century, Abbot Aelfric translated parts of the Old Testament.

Here's Aelfric's first line in his account of the Tower of Babel:

"Aefter thaem sothlice ealle menn spraecon any spraece."

And he didn't misspell one word!

As the twelfth century was turning into the thirteenth an Augustinian monk named Orm, or Ormin, put together a poetical version of the Gospels and Acts of the Apostles.

About fifty years later Genesis and Exodus were put into rhyme. Yet children didn't memorize it. Adults didn't discuss Moses over a morning bowl of porridge. The ordinary man shuffling down a narrow London street didn't know Job from Joshua.

Today the situation isn't much different. Most people haven't the foggiest notion what the Bible says. Yet at least the Englishmen during the Middle Ages had no choice. We do.

Before we discuss how John Wycliffe helped introduce the Bible to his barber, baker, and tailor, we might probe the society in which he lived. If you think *you've* got it rough when your electric blanket goes on the blink, just check this out . . .

Peasants, during the end of the Middle Ages and during the Reformation, huddled up in cottages of timber, clay, and rubble with a roof of thatch and an earthen floor. Real cozy.

Out of the peasant's earnings he paid a "great tithe," or tenth, of his grain, a tenth of his fruit, vegetables, and livestock. He paid a fixed percentage of his income to his "lord" twice a year.

Just when the crops were ready to haul in, a peasant's lord might call him for up to sixty days of personal service. This might include harvesting wheat, scrubbing walls, or beating the bushes for game while the lord was on a hunt.

Hungry men were often forced to poach—killing quail, pheasant, doves, and deer which belonged to the lord. The penalty for poaching left its impression by way of cut-off hands or gouged-out eyes.

Please—don't ask about the church. No use suggesting these peasants grab a free meal at their local prayer meeting or simply apply for the church welfare roll.

The church was as distant to the common man as was God. And God was successfully brushed aside by the leaders of the monasteries and universities who would rather argue about how many locusts John the Baptist ate daily than about what Jesus said about salvation.

And although this subject of salvation was

argued by the scholars (and still is among theologians of various shapes and sizes) the poor working man could only relate to weird cults, weird miracles, and weird pagan beliefs.

Did we say the backward Middle Ages? Yes, of course. In our present age of "enlightenment" we don't go in for astrology, ouija boards, witchcraft, and sorcery. Or do we . . .?

By the time the twelfth century rolled around, Mother Mary hit popular religion. People worshiped her. She was all love, all kindness, and the way to get a free ticket into heaven.

The masses of people were afraid of God—scared stiff of that cosmic tyrant who might turn them into ashes with his breath if they ever approached him directly with a request.

Of course, Jesus told it another way, but why get picky?

"For he longs for all to be saved and to understand this truth," Paul wrote about Jesus, "that God is on one side and all the people on the other side, and Christ Jesus, himself man, is between them to bring them together" (1 Timothy 2:4, 5).

One mediator. Jesus. And he becomes concerned when someone steps in between himself and his children. But the people of the Middle Ages were so ignorant of Scripture it's easy to understand how they could have been misled.

With the Bible as best seller in today's world

there are no more problems, right? Anyway . .

Those of us who have discovered that God is alive and Jesus is real know the Bible is relevant. We can understand why, back in the fourteenth century, John Wycliffe became upset with the system of his generation.

Big John knew that the key to life was in a Book the masses weren't reading. He knew his God wasn't selfish, keeping himself stashed away on a top shelf in a university library.

Now for a brief account of how John Wycliffe helped to shatter his church establishment and bring God to life for a dead civilization.

4

The Restless Wycliffe

The details of John Wycliffe's early life are so obscure that those who could tell you the minute of his death couldn't agree on when he was born. Most guess between 1320 and 1330.

Wycliffe was raised in the North Riding of Yorkshire, England. After he arrived at Oxford University in 1346 he began to clash emotionally, intellectually, and spiritually with the church establishment.

Over the years Wycliffe's feelings moved rapidly from thought to action.

His name has been academically linked to three colleges: Queen's, Merton, and Balliol. Between 1356 and 1360 Wycliffe was elected the third Master (we'd say Dean) of Balliol, a position which he resigned a year later. Very restless.

Initially Wycliffe played the church game by the church rules. He's said to have become a chaplain to the king in 1366—kind of a prestige part-time job while he continued his studies.

He earned his bachelor's degree in 1369 and his doctor of theology degree in 1372. At this time Wycliffe still maintained a relationship with the era's only Church, from the Pope on down.

In 1373 Pope Gregory XI renewed Wycliffe's financial grant, although it's doubtful he ever received it, and in 1374 Wycliffe split for France to rap with papal authorities about filling church leadership roles in England.

A few years later the real fun began. In 1377 Wycliffe began to preach from various pulpits in London, attacking the hierarchy of clerks and the wealthy clergy.

This made him an immediate enemy to Courtenay, bishop of London, and his timid friend Sudbury, archbishop of Canterbury. Wycliffe was ordered to appear before them both at St. Paul's Cathedral in 1377 but they were so disorganized they couldn't make their charges stick, and Wycliffe walked away uncondemned.

The London grapevine reached down to Rome where the Pope, three months later, issued five "bulls" against Wycliffe. No, not the "toro" type, charging him in a small ring. It just means the Pope was very, very unhappy with Wycliffe, and issued written reprimands.

In 1378 the great split occurred within the Catholic church. Both Gregory XI and Urban VI claimed to be pope. Wycliffe said the dispute reminded him of two dogs fighting over a bone.

From August 1380 until the summer of 1381 Wycliffe hung out in his rooms at Queen's, writing, studying, and continuing a most revolutionary thing: translating the Bible into an English language the average man could understand.

Wycliffe organized a group of itinerant preachers to travel from village to village telling the people the simple message of God's love.

The church's hatred became directed, in part, against these preachers whom they dubbed "Lollards," which some say meant "idle babblers."

That year of 1381 saw the Peasant's Revolt, a rather bloody revolution which helped unite the church and state together against their common enemy, the uneducated masses of restless lower class citizens.

Wycliffe's writings, unread by the masses, didn't cause the revolt. Yet his known sympathies with the peasants against the prim and proper

clergy helped bring resentment against himself to a full boil.

During the fighting, Sudbury, that shy bishop, was murdered. The ambitious Courtenay quickly filled his shoes and took action against Wycliffe.

After Wycliffe was deemed a heretic, his friends were forced to argue against his theology and his writings were banned. In 1382 Wycliffe was kicked out of Oxford. A few months later, he suffered his first stroke, which left him partly paralyzed. Soon he retired to his parish at Lutterworth. More than two years later Wycliffe was conducting mass at Lutterworth when another severe stroke struck him down.

John Wycliffe died three days later, on December 31, 1384.

On thousands of tombstones there is written "R.I.P."—"Rest in peace." After being hassled his whole life, ridiculed, laughed at, despised, hated, and condemned by his church, you might think a dead John Wycliffe would be left alone.

Not so.

In 1482, *one hundred years later*, Richard Fleming, bishop of Lincoln, carried out an order of the Council of Constance. Fleming grabbed a shovel, dug up poor Wycliffe's bones, burnt them, and threw the ashes into the river Swift.

The trial of John Wycliffe

It's a fair guess to assume that Wycliffe didn't feel a thing. Besides, the opinions of this man and the English Bible which he had helped to translate had already left a growing scar in the face of centuries-old tradition.

What was it he said? Was the church really all that rotten? How could so many giants of religion get so uptight with one Oxford scholar? If you can't answer in twenty words or less then read on . . .

Here's the way it was. The church leaders were diplomats, administrators, and economists while finding little time to spend on such materially unrewarding things as spiritual matters.

That's like some dude today studying business administration, accounting, and political science to get ready to be a preacher.

Thirteen of twenty-five bishops in England and Wales between 1376 and 1386 held high offices in the king's service and many of the others weren't strangers to the men who ran the country.

So in many dioceses the clergy were fat and lazy, corrupt or controlled, allowing buildings to fall apart and ignoring the needs of the poor peasants.

Priests and cardinals were also guilty of working for the wrong king, ignoring the King of kings, who could deliver so much more than gold rings or a three-year warranty on an air-conditioned carriage.

John Wycliffe didn't just say, "Naughty, naughty," and let it go at that.

"The clergy are said to have regal palaces, houses and churches, excessive in size, in subtlety, in costliness and with glittering ornaments for decoration," Wycliffe wrote.

"They have overmuch wealth," he continued, "both in great wasteful houses, in precious clothes, in great feasts and many jewels and treasures." Somehow Wycliffe couldn't mesh the clergy's life style with the one outlined in the New Testament.

"Don't store your profits here on earth where they can erode away or may be stolen," Jesus told the people. "Store them in heaven where they will never lose their value, and are safe from thieves! If your profits are in heaven your heart will be there too" ((Matthew 6:19-21).

What this means is that those who have become children of God by belief in Jesus may throw some coins into an eternal vault. They can have treasures which will last forever, simply by obeying their King and allowing him to live through their lives.

Not only didn't the clergy give God a chance to take care of them but they openly begged and solicited funds from the already poor peasants. The thought of drinking a cheap grade of champagne must have been too much to bear . . .

O.K. We'll be as fair as possible. Although

most of the church was pretty far out of it there were those friars who did minister to the poor. Some preaching was effective and scriptural. There were some honest attempts at charity. Yet this happened less from the leadership of the church than from the faith of individuals who were, simply, Christians—Christians in the sense that they, like Wycliffe, sought the guidance of their Lord above the ramblings of man. Once they got to know the person of Christ their generosity and compassion were a result of their relationship with him instead of religious obligation.

Wycliffe is best known for the Bible associated with his name. Although there were already translations of some parts of the Bible in English during his time, a complete translation had not been completed before he started his campaign.

He completely broke with tradition by proposing that the entire Scriptures be made available in the vernacular. He wanted a Bible which wasn't weighed down with Latin, a Bible which any literate man could read.

"Every Christian," Wycliffe said, "ought to study this book because it is the whole truth. Christ and his apostles taught the people in that tongue that was best known to them. Why should men not do so now?" Wycliffe's translations came from the Latin Vulgate. Remember Jerome? To go from Hebrew and Greek into

Latin and then into English resulted in a text which wasn't close enough to the original. There's an old cliche—"It loses something in the translation." Then if there's more loss through another translation . . . wow!

One version of Wycliffe's Bible followed the Latin grammar and syntax word for word, which often produced nonsensical passages.

A second version, also from the Latin Vulgate and therefore similar to the first, was written in a looser style, more idiomatic and with fewer grammatical tangles.

Wycliffe himself wrote several books and articles in Latin or English, leaving him little time to share in the burden of the translation. No one denies he inspired the whole project and from the very beginning his name was tied to it.

The translators were hand-picked from Oxford and are credited with inserting as little doctrinal prejudice as possible. They were merely concerned with telling it the way it was written so the masses could read the Bible and grasp its truth.

Some scholars believe Wycliffe was more concerned with educating the less-learned clergy and educated laymen than he was in reaching the entire population. But even this was a radical step away from tradition.

Tradition, in Wycliffe's day, was considered

in the same bag as the Scriptures. Medieval students in the church saw little difference between what the apostles said and what the church dictated. Wycliffe always went to extremes to separate the two. He insisted that Christian truth and practice be based on God's Word rather than church ritual. He placed Scripture higher than the Pope's head—and that's when the trouble started.

Wycliffe actually had the nerve to suggest that priests should read the Scriptures and preach sermons from them! How's that for revolutionary?

At first Wycliffe believed that reason and church leaders could point believers to the meaning of Scripture, but later came to agree with Jesus that God himself could handle it.

"But I will send you the Comforter, the Holy Spirit," Jesus told his followers, "the source of all truth. He will come to you from the Father and will tell you all about me" (John 15:26).

He didn't mean there was anything wrong with teachers, just that a believer could count on God's Spirit to reveal truth through the Scriptures as well as give a guy good or bad vibes about what was being taught by men.

"One part of Scripture explains another," Wycliffe wrote, and added that every text must be understood in context with the whole truth of the Bible.

Yet even today there are any number of cults

and splinters from the biblical plank based on isolated passages from Scripture. You can support almost any kind of weird trip by using the Bible as a reference—as long as you don't use too many verses or study the entire message at hand.

While Wycliffe's bones were at rest (before the bonfire), his followers scattered the new English translation throughout England. Only the wealthy could afford to buy a Bible, since each was copied by hand (printing was unknown). The owners shared their Bibles with those less fortunate than themselves, or else recited memorized verses for all to hear.

Wycliffe's Bible became popular in such a short time that the church began to sweat a little under the pressure. Finally Archbishop Arundel complained to the Pope about ". . . that pestilent wretch, John Wycliffe, who has invented a new translation of the Scriptures." Soon thereafter the head man at Canterbury forbade use of the Wycliffe Bible under penalty of excommunication. Leaders of Christian countries were urged to execute anyone following the beliefs of Wycliffe.

For the true believers excommunication wasn't hard to take. They knew Jesus said once you're his, you're his. Period. No man-made institution could ever rip a believer from God's hand.

As far as death goes, the true believers knew it'd only hurt for a little while. Perhaps they read what the Apostle Paul had to say on the subject: "Sometimes I want to live and at other times I don't, for I long to go and be with Christ. How much happier for me than being here!" (Philippians 1:23).

Heads we win, tails they lose.

In England things got a little hot. Old King Henry IV passed a law for Wycliffe's fellow heretics which—quite mercifully—would only fine and imprison first offenders. If a believer came through the courts a *second* time and was convicted of being a heretic, he wasn't fined or imprisoned at all. He was merely taken to a public square and burned to death.

It seems the old king couldn't burn enough people, for Wycliffe's translation spread rapidly; the average man became more and more familiar with the Scriptures—and the church hierarchy was making aspirin their national food.

It isn't that Wycliffe was so much a revolutionary, historians say, as he was a reformer. Very subtle hints have been made in this chapter, as you know, as to what items might have needed reforming.

Just one year after Wycliffe's ashes did a backstroke down the Swift, a baby was born in Europe who would *really* show the people what reform was all about.

Martin Luther.

Wycliffe's translators worked fifteen years, finished their Bible shortly before their leader died, and then laid in a big supply of quill pens to make copies for the public. However, when Luther finished *his* work a neat little invention waited to affect history. The printing press.

And when the first ink-smeared printer yelled, "Hit it!" he didn't know the few splashes made by Wycliffe would seem like nothing, compared to Luther's worldwide tidal wave.

5

Rebellion Against Rome

That Bible of the Middle Ages was a rare book indeed. Frightfully expensive, old boy. And it wasn't something you could check out for two weeks from Ye Olde Publick Library.

We've all become terribly spoiled in this century. After all, just open up your mail on an average day and you'll receive stacks of worthless literature beyond your wildest imagination.

This is due, of course, to a quaint little invention perfected around 1440 by Johann Gutenberg of Mainz, Germany. It was this mechanical device which allowed the entire Reformation movement to explode rather than fizzle into oblivion.

Gutenberg didn't have a chance to run off a quick photostat of his writings, borrow a neighbor's mimeograph machine, or even ask his secretary to make three carbon copies of a letter.

All he could do was ask her if she had writer's cramp. For that was the only way, back then. You wrote. Period. Keep dipping that scratchy quill pen in the messy ink and write.

Then Gutenberg developed the amazing technique of setting individual letters in lines and coating them with an oil-based ink. He used a screw-and-lever press to slam one sheet of paper at a time against the type. Terribly clever.

The fifteenth century thereby gave birth to the first industry involving mass production. More books were printed in thirty years than had been copied by hand over several centuries.

Major cities rapidly acquired several presses and *boom*—all of a sudden millions of literate citizens were able to read pamphlets and books on various subjects never revealed to them before.

The clergy and the very rich began to get an uncomfortable itch beneath their stiff, intellectual collars.

To fully grasp the impact printing had on society just picture yourself using tin cans and string to speak to some dude standing a hundred feet away. You speak loudly and struggle to make out his reply. Then some clown comes along and installs something you've never seen before. A telephone. Presto! You can speak in normal tones to the dude's brother living a thousand miles away.

Now the masses could have a constant flow of ideas to read instead of hanging on to Aunt Hilda's three-year-old letter as their only example of the written word.

Before the printing press destroyed the demand for scribes, professional copiers would spend four or five months on a 200-page text. Besides the scribe's cost, twenty-five sheep got the swift ax so their skins could be used for the text's parchment.

Cheaper books were made by using carved words and pictures on single wood blocks, inking them and, by hand, pressing the block to a piece of paper to form a page. The results were messy and not cheap enough to produce a large enough quantity.

Gutenberg's movable type did the trick—individual metal letters you could set and reset. He chased out the bugs of messiness and expense and he was all ready to print the biggie. The Bible.

Gutenberg's German Bible was printed in a heavy, rough-edged Gothic face which resembled 15th-century German penmanship. Not the easiest thing to read. Near the end of the century

an easier-to-read roman type took over most of the world.

The less expensive products of the press sold out as soon as the ink was dry. Martin Luther's German Bible swept through 430 editions in his lifetime and peasants spent a few pennies each on Luther's propaganda sheets and on those attacking him.

Hold it! Who's this Luther fellow? What's he have to do with Gutenberg and the printer's union? Very simply, Luther was one of the first to make use of the printing press to get the people together for a religious happening called the Reformation.

For Luther it all started in 1483 when he was born in the mining town of Eisleben in Saxony (Germany). Before we hop back to England we'll take a snappy look at Luther and some of his activist friends.

When Luther was growing up the people were growing out. Out of darkness. Out of fear. Out of gloom. Widespread education brought to the masses by the printing press, a newly dynamic economy, plus reexamination of the church institution worked together to set the stage for Luther's manipulation of movable type.

Luther's parents became very uptight when

Martin Luther

61

he dropped out of law school and retreated to a monastery. Martin wanted peace of mind and spiritual grace.

When he was twenty-two, in 1505, Luther entered the Augustinian cloister at Erfurt. This was one of the strictest monasteries; most others were being attacked for the monks' loose living and hoarding of wealth.

Luther was soon labeled a fanatic for the way in which he fasted, prayed, and studied long into the night. Luther said later that if he had continued with this life style he would have killed himself.

The monks sent him off to the University of Wittenberg in 1508 where Luther taught moral philosophy and Christian theology. He was well respected, but personally he still felt an annoying emptiness within him which he couldn't fill with religion.

Two years later he walked eight hundred miles to Rome where he fell to the ground and cried out, "Hail, Holy Rome!" His loyalties were still intact.

Luther was disappointed with the stories he heard in Rome about the cardinals and popes. Their graft and pleasures were common knowledge. Yet he passed this off as a fault of the system and went back to Wittenberg to study for his doctorate. It wasn't long before one of his professors remarked: "This monk

(Luther) will confuse all the doctors. He will start a new religion and reform the whole Roman Church, for he bases his theology on the writings of the prophets and the apostles."

(Tch, tch. Can't do that!)

In Luther's day the church was like a giant state with no specific territory. It had government officials in the Pope, cardinals and priests—legislative bodies in ecumenical councils—canon law—courts—and financial agencies. It went to war, signed treaties, and collected taxes.

The biggest hang-up the church had was in collecting money from the peasants. Tons of coin poured into the church treasury as leaders promised the people forgiveness for particular sins, depending on how much bread the sinner would toss into the church vault.

"But if we confess our sins to him (God, not the church)," John wrote, "he can be depended on to forgive us and to cleanse us from every wrong. And it is perfectly proper for God to do this for us because Christ died to wash away our sins" (1 John 1:9).

It's a whole lot cheaper, too . . . for us. It was very costly for Jesus.

As Luther became more and more troubled about church operations, the Holy Spirit guided him to a passage in Scripture which changed everything for him.

"The just shall live by faith," Paul wrote. Wow!

Luther had always thought he didn't deserve salvation and couldn't figure out a way to buy it. With this new revelation he saw that God's love, grace, *and* salvation were free gifts. In protest to the church's seeking payment for forgiveness of sins, Luther decided to do what other scholars were doing: post his ideas in a public place.

On October 31, 1517, Luther tacked up his ninety-five theses for debate on the door of the Castle Church in Wittenberg. Thousands identified with Luther's thoughts and within a few months his theses were spread all over Europe—again, thanks to the printing press.

As the years went on the tempers got shorter and the Reformation broader. In 1529 Luther stated that since the church would not reform itself the secular authorities should do it for them.

Thumping the New Testament as his basis for doctrine, Luther slammed head-on into Rome by declaring that during the past thousand years the Church had taken Christ's words and twisted them to its own liking.

In a few cities the local politicians loyal to Rome were able to burn Luther's books, but on December 10, 1520, Luther and his students returned the favor by burning the church's hallowed *Canon Law* in a great public bonfire.

The *Edict of Worms* in 1521 finally declared

Luther an outlaw and the reformer split for Wartburg, a mountain fortress, to lie low for almost a year.

Other leaders of the protest soon started doctrinal fires burning the seat of Rome. Ulrich Zwingli, born in 1484 in Switzerland, was ordained as a priest in 1506.

He began to study Greek at the age of twenty-nine so he could read the New Testament in its original language. Six years later, in 1519, he began his own reform movement in Zurich. He was pretty wrapped up in a humanist trip he had come across at the Universities of Vienna and Basle, leading him to try to raise the moral standards of his congregation and point them directly to the Scriptures rather than defy the organized church.

The Pope had lost so many Germans to Luther that he didn't want a second feature playing in Switzerland. He left Zwingli alone. But Luther didn't.

That's right. The dude who had preached against religious narrow-mindedness and religious ritual and ceremony now attacked Zwingli. For as Luther pushed ahead through middle age he began to practice tedious services and traditions he had once thrown out.

After awhile, the Pope had to deal with Zwingli . . . and how! A small Swiss army of 8,000 Catholics faced off with Zwingli's 1,500 troops in 1531. Zwingli's men were slain or scattered and as night fell, the reformer was found under a pear tree by his enemies, who promptly sent him to join his King.

With Zwingli dead and Luther beginning to play out, the eyes of the masses turned to Geneva. There they found John Calvin.

Calvin was born in 1509 in northern France. He studied for the priesthood, quit that to pursue law, and then got hung up on Greek philosophers who exalted strict personal discipline.

Eventually he rapped with reformers for long periods of time, which resulted in his writing *The Institutes of the Christian Religion*, a defense of the reform movement and a detailed theological instruction manual.

Calvin stopped in Geneva on a trip, intending to stay just one night, but wound up living there the rest of his life. To be as fair as possible to Calvin, let it be said he set up a Genevan dictatorship, a theocratic state, which was far harsher than the Catholic Church had imposed.

Some 16th-century activists in Geneva named their dogs "Calvin" or called Calvin "Cain," but the price was heavy: their lives or expulsion from the city. That's what you get when you replace one bummer with another instead of letting God's grace replace man's greed. Still, Calvin's theology has endured and has a strong influence on Christianity as we know it today.

John Knox eventually exported Calvinism to Scotland. The Anabaptists rose up in Zurich in 1525, separating themselves from the secular state and allowing—above other groups—true freedom of worship.

Luther, Zwingli, Calvin and their other contemporaries were divided by national loyalties and personal hang-ups but were united in their faith in Scripture, God's free grace, and rebellion against Rome.

Swim back across the English Channel for a while to the foggy island and consider this: As we entered the 16th century there was still no complete English Bible translated from the original Hebrew and Greek. Wycliffe was stuck with Latin, remember? So it appears the good Lord pushed some clouds apart with his hands and began a work which shook up the English world by shouting down to earth:

"You there, William Tyndale!"

"Yes, Lord?"

"Have I got some heavy work to lay on you!"

The Trials of Tyndale

William Tyndale was born in Gloucestershire, England, about 1492—the same time Columbus went searching for India and about a decade and a half before John Calvin was born. He shoved his nose into the books and came up with a Bachelor of Arts degree in 1512 from Oxford and followed this with a Master's in 1515. He lectured in local schools for a year before moving to Cambridge.

The great Greek scholar Erasmus had probably left Cambridge a couple of years before Tyndale arrived. However, the studious and curious Tyndale lost no time in flipping through Erasmus' Greek Testament.

What started out as an academic exercise turned into a revelation of God's Word for Tyndale. Over and over again he pored over the Greek Scriptures, digging in and asking questions and receiving answers about God's plan. for man.

The local priests became upset when this young scholar constantly pressured them to read the Scriptures for themselves. One church clergyman finally said: "We had better be without God's laws than the Pope's."

"I defy the Pope and all his laws," Tyndale shot back, "and if God spare me I will one day make the boy that drives the plow in England to know more of Scripture than the Pope himself!"

Hah!

Tyndale took himself seriously enough to begin translating the original Greek into English. He asked Cuthbert Tonstal, bishop of London, if he could use a couple of rooms in the bishop's huge palace for office space. The bishop claimed to be vastly interested in learning and all that, but really! House a man who would choose God over the Pope? Be serious . . .

William Tyndale

Yet the Lord comes through when man doesn't. A wealthy merchant named Humphrey Monmouth put Tyndale up in his London home and let the scholar begin his translating. It wasn't as peaceful as he would have liked, for by just glancing out of a window Tyndale could see men being led off to prison or execution for merely owning or reading a copy of Luther's writings.

What would they do when a *Bible* translation came out?

Tyndale didn't stick around long enough to find out. He decided that no place in England was safe enough for such a dangerous work.

He split for Hamburg, Germany. Tyndale was hunted, hungry and flat broke. Yet he plugged along day and night, translating from Greek to English. Tyndale drove himself so hard that the next year he carried handwritten sheets containing the New Testament in English to a printer in Cologne. He knew if he could get this translation printed there'd be no stopping him.

Yet often just before God's able to lay a really heavy victory on a Christian there are times of extreme trial and testing. Just as Tyndale reached the peak of his hopes the church establishment came crashing down. It seems a priest named Cochlaeus had caught an earful while overhearing printers discuss their latest projects. He bought enough wine for the printers to get them sloppy drunk and tongues started wagging.

Tyndale's well-kept secret was suddenly public knowledge. The priest learned the truth: An English New Testament was in the press and almost finished. He reported this to the magistrates, who demanded the sheets be seized and then warned the English bishops of this new threat to the Pope's rigid rule.

Tyndale was a step and a half ahead of the officials as he heard what had happened, rushed in panic to the printer's, and grabbed whatever sheets he could find.

He escaped to Worms, Luther's old German stronghold on the Rhine, where public support of the Reformation remained solid. There, for the first time in history, a *printed* New Testament in English was produced.

Tyndale turned smuggler. He knew Big Brother would be waiting in England to smash any attempt to bring that annoying new text into the country, so he printed up a small edition—for hiding. And hide them he did. Tyndale took his tiny Bible and shoved copies into boxes, bales of cloth, wooden barrels, and sacks of grain and flour. The cargo was then placed on board ship and taken to the English ports.

Man—you talk about the scriptural egg hitting the establishment fan! Where Wycliffe's boys could only turn out a copy of his Bible every few months or so, which were purchased mainly by the very rich, Tyndale's little product really shook things up. Hundreds upon hundreds were printed each day and could easily be bought by the man in the street. British troops were assigned to the ports for the specific purpose of finding these dangerous little books. Thousands were discovered and brought to St. Paul's Cross in London, where the clergy held a "burnt offering most pleasing to Almighty God."

God must not have been too pleased by the smoke for he kept Tyndale in business printing thousands more.

"In burning the book they did none other thing than I looked for," Tyndale said. "No more shall they do if they burn me also, if it be God's will that it should be so."

You can't mess around with God once he makes up his mind . . .

Tonstal, the same bishop of London who had refused to house Tyndale, now sought another way of wiping out his opponent. He simply couldn't prevent hundreds of Bibles from slipping through customs.

Tonstal approached Augustine Pakington, a merchant who traded to Antwerp, Belgium, and suggested a rather smashing idea. The bishop would very smoothly have Pakington *buy* every copy of Tyndale's book in Europe and thereby be rid of the whole business.

Their conversation is recorded historically as follows:

74

"My lord," Pakington replied, "if it be your pleasure I could do in this matter probably more than any merchant in England; so if it be your lordship's desire to pay for them—for I must disburse money for them—I will be sure to get for you every book that remains unsold."

"Good Master Pakington," the bishop grinned, "do your diligence and get them for me, and I will gladly give you whatever they may cost, for the books are naughty, and I intend surely to destroy them all, and to burn them at St. Paul's Cross."

Now the plot gets thicker. Unknown to the bishop, Pakington was a friend of Tyndale. He split for Europe and found Tyndale in his tiny room.

"Master Tyndale," Pakington said, "I have found you a good purchaser for your books."

"Who is he?"

"My lord bishop of London."

"But if the bishop wants the books it must be only to burn them," Tyndale answered.

"Well, what of it?" Pakington winked. "The bishop will burn them anyhow, and it is best that you should have the money to print others to take their place."

Tyndale could have laughed all the way to the bank. He made enough bread on the sale to correct his first edition of its errors and then print thousands of new copies. The bishop bought at retail and Tyndale printed at wholesale.

England became flooded with waves of new Tyndale translations. When Tonstal asked how this could possibly have happened, Pakington merely suggested he could do nothing more without destroying the printing plates. This was never done.

Tonstal switched tactics. He preached a sermon at St. Paul's Cross in which he called Tyndale's New Testament "naughty" and declared it contained two thousand errors. After Tyndale defended these attacks in writing it became apparent the two thousand errors had somehow dwindled down to perhaps six possible mistranslations of Greek words.

Tyndale was living in the house of a close friend in Antwerp, an English merchant named Pointz. For years the church had been trying to physically get rid of Tyndale. Near the end of 1534 the king hired two men to succeed where others had failed. Henry Phillips, a smooth-talking con-man, played the part of a "gentleman." Gabriel Donne, an English monk, played the part of Phillips' servant.

Phillips gradually talked his way into Tyndale's confidence and managed to become another boarder in Pointz' home. After several lengthy conversations about the church and theology, amateur private eye Phillips decided he had enough evidence against Tyndale. He tried to get the Antwerp city government to arrest the famous translator but the town supported Tyndale. Thirty miles away, in Brussels, Phillips talked the emperor's attorney into traveling to Antwerp and arresting Tyndale.

The attorney chickened out when he saw the solid support for Tyndale in the town and the large political influence of the English merchants.

Phillips waited and waited. He seized his opportunity when Pointz left town for a while. A group of the sheriff's men waited at the door while Phillips marched up to Tyndale's room to borrow forty shillings. He told the scholar that he had lost his purse. Tyndale didn't hesitate. He gave the coins to Phillips who, jingling Tyndale's money, offered to buy him dinner. Big-hearted treat!

Tyndale insisted on taking Phillips out to dinner, and as they left the house Phillips ducked behind Tyndale to let him go first. As they neared the sheriff's men, Phillips pointed to Tyndale's back and the game was over. He was rushed to the dungeons of the castle of Vilvorde, eighteen miles from Antwerp. There he rotted away, wrapping thin rags around himself as his friends tried in vain to free him.

For two years Tyndale remained a prisoner. Not unlike the Apostle Paul, also a long-term prisoner in his day, Tyndale asked for books and study material. He determined to continue his study of the Hebrew Old Testament and its translation.

Curious how Tyndale's English compares to ours? Try the Lord's Prayer on for size:

"O oure father, which art in heven halowed by thy name. Let thy kyngdom come. Thy wyll be fulfilled, as well in erth, as hit ys in heven. Geve vs this daye oure dayly breade. And forgeve vs oure treaspases, even as we forgeve them whych treaspas vs. Lede vs nott in to temptacion, but delyvre vs from yvell, Amen."

Swift, eh? Tyndale's translation was much closer to the original Greek than Luther's. He based it on Erasmus' third printed edition of the Greek Testament which came out in 1522.

Tyndale was obviously concerned with his translation's clarity. No use being picky about everything if the people can't understand it. He used good English, not literal Greek idioms.

He devoted himself mostly to the New Testament, managing only to translate the five books of Moses, the historical books, and part of the prophets in the Old Testament's original Hebrew.

Friday, October 6, 1536. The court of Brussels had already condemned Tyndale, and it was time to carry out their decision. The pale-faced prisoner was led to a public square and tied firmly to a stake. The hangman didn't offer him a last meal or cigarette. He didn't even whip out a blindfold to dangle in front of his victim. He just placed his hands around Tyndale's throat and strangled him.

In case there was any doubt, his body was then burned to ashes. The last words Tyndale spoke were in a piercing, loud voice: "Lord, open the king of England's eyes!"

Without getting into a study of the king's eyes, let it be said that the Reformation was well planted. Only three years after Tyndale was so rudely interrupted, King Henry VIII no longer opposed a "people's Bible."

Seventy years after Tyndale's death, good old King James hopped on the Reformation band-wagon of translations to do his own kind of thing.

Go ahead. Read about the King James version, the most well known of all. Then try to figure out why so many modern Christians still think today's date is 1611.

God's Silly Vassal and the KJV

King James VI of Scotland had been ruling for thirty-seven years when Queen Elizabeth of England, taking care of business on the other part of the island, died on March 24, 1603. So James VI quickly dropped his "V" and headed south to become James I—of England. A definite royal promotion. Fringe benefits, sick leave, all that . . . .

January, 1604. The good king called the Hampton Court Conference in answer to a group of very uptight Puritans who were at odds with the English church, which by this time had broken with Rome. James was more interested in politics than religion, regarding himself as being above such trivial things as doctrines. Yet, wishing to please his new subjects, he called the conference.

Royal rudeness prevailed at the meeting and not much good came of it. With one historic exception: John Reynolds, the Puritan president of Corpus Christi College, Oxford, suggested an authorized version of the English Bible be written in order to please all factions within the church.

Although many present disagreed with this idea, it was immediately pounced upon by peace-maker James, who saw it as a way to ease tempers.

"I profess," James said, "I could never yet see a Bible well translated in English; but I think that, of all, that of Geneva is the worst. I wish some special pains were taken for an uniform translation, which should be done by the best-learned men in both Universities, then reviewed by the Bishops, presented to the Privy Council, lastly ratified by Royal authority, to be read in the whole Church, and none other."

This Geneva Bible was actually one of the best to that date and was considered the home Bible. The Bible used in churches was the Bishops' Bible. James objected to the Geneva translation not so much for the way the Scripture came out but because the marginal notes offended his ego. He had always believed kings were appointed by God to govern the people by divine right, and some notes in the Geneva Bible didn't agree with this. He said they were "very partial, untrue, seditious, and savouring too much of dangerous and traitorous conceits."

James cited two examples. The Geneva Bible stated the Hebrew midwives were right to disobey the Egyptian king's orders (Exodus 1:19) and the mother of King Asa should have been beheaded for being an idolator (2 Chronicles 15:16). James thought this last comment might bring a negative reaction to the memory of his own mother, Mary Queen of Scots.

Therefore James ordered a translation which would "embody the best in the existing versions and which could be read both in the public services of the Church and in homes by private individuals."

Six companies of men, totaling forty-seven translators, were appointed to begin work on the new version. Two companies met at Cambridge to revise 1 Chronicles through Ecclesiastes, and the Apocrypha. At Oxford two other companies were to revise Isaiah through Malachi, the four Gospels, Acts, and the Apocalypse. The last group, at Westminster, revised Genesis through 2 Kings and Romans through Jude.

James instructed this group of well-known Bible scholars to use the Bishops' Bible as the basis for the new translation. He also told them to use names in common usage, such as "Isaac." Geneva had used "Izhak" and the Bishops' called him "Isahac."

They neglected to establish a thread of common usage between both Testaments. The prophet Elijah in the Old Testament comes out as *Elias* in the New. And twice the New Testament refers to the Old Testament leader Joshua as "Jesus." "Jesus" is, in fact, the Greek for Joshua, but the variation did confuse things.

The new version used no marginal notes, thereby offending no one, and explained only original Hebrew or Greek words when necessary.

The Bishops' Bible was last printed in 1606. The Authorized Version, or King James Version (KJV) as we say in America, competed with the Puritan's Geneva Bible for a while. Yet the smooth, splendid style of the new version eventually wiped out the Geneva in the popularity polls and in the book stalls.

Even today many believers feel you must say "thou" and "thee" in order to stay under God's grace. They overlook the fact that "thee" and "thou" was the common, everyday speech of the people of King James' day, and that the parallel "you" is just as meaningful today. We believe the Lord has always had this thing about speaking simply to the people, even as Paul wrote:

"Dear brothers, even when I first came to you I didn't use lofty words and brilliant ideas to tell you God's message. And my preaching was very plain, not with a lot of oratory and human wisdom, but the Holy Spirit's power was in my words, proving to those who heard them that the message was from God" (1 Corinthians 2:1, 4). A Spirit job rather than a snow job.

When the KJV finally was printed, the title page read:

The Holy Bible, Conteyning the Old Testament and the New: Newly Translated out of the Originall tongues, with the former Translations diligently compared and revised, by his Majesties speciall commandment. Appointed to be read in Churches. Imprinted at London by Robert Barker, Printer to the Kings most Excellent Majestie. Anna Dom. 1611.

Some scholars doubt the KJV was actually authorized by any king or council, but the words "Appointed to be read in Churches" indicates at least some kind of formal OK. It seemed possible to later critics that the government council did give the new version an official green light, but records of the council between 1600 and 1613 were destroyed by fire in 1618.

King James basked in the glory of his new version. Although it largely ignored the most accurate texts of the twelfth to fifteenth centuries, the new Bible became greatly in demand.

Previously, while James was reigning in Scotland, a Scottish churchman called him "God's silly vassal" and informed him that although James was number one in Scotland's kingdom he was only an average member of the kingdom of Christ. You can imagine James' ecstasy when his translators dedicated the new version of the Bible to "the most high and mighty prince James."

The "mighty prince" saw his Bible take off for many reasons. The group of famous scholars translating the work didn't hurt things any and the different groups backing the effort helped establish a broad base of support.

The religious vibes were good in those days with most of the serious translating having already been done, beginning with Tyndale (the original Greek and Hebrew).

Printers who zipped out one edition of the KJV were in such a hurry to fill up the window of the local book store that they made a few mistakes. For example:

In 1631 the word "not" was left out of the seventh of the Ten Commandments, so this was called the "Wicked Bible." The "Vinegar Bible" was printed in 1717 because the chapter heading of Luke 20 read "vinegar" instead of "vineyard."

In 1795 the printer slipped in "killed" instead of "filled" in Mark 7:27 and unknowingly produced the "Murderer's Bible."

Archbishop Ussher used his influence to have his series of biblical dates, setting creation at 4004 B.C., inserted in 1701 editions and they have remained to this date, although the early dates are guesses and not fact. Ussher's speculations have encouraged constant debate between believers and nonbelievers and also among Christians themselves, as if they were a part of the real text.

Dr. Paris of Cambridge in 1762 and Dr. Blayney of Oxford in 1769 revised the Authorized Version in its spelling and grammar. It's said Blayney's edition differs from the 1611 original in about 75,000 details. This edition is still used by vast numbers of Protestant Christians today.

Keep in mind the KJV was a giant step forward in the "Mother, May I?" game of Bible translations. Its readability, in its day, and ready availability for the working man pushed it ahead of any other work.

Many believers discover no matter how many times they read a particular bit of Scripture there's always a deeper meaning, a new spiritual truth which God can teach you. As we uncover manuscripts closer and closer to the original texts we almost feel a stronger and stronger pulse from the Lord's heartbeat.

In the first chapters of this book we discussed the Dead Sea Scrolls as being one example of man's recent discovery of ancient copies of Scripture. Recently even more fragments of parchment are being dusted off from their centuries-old resting places.

So we ask you: If a soft drink tastes better to you on a hot, muggy day, than water—how much better a root beer float?

"Huh?" you might well ask. OK. If the King James Version was superior to earlier works, fine. Yet if archeologists dig their fingers into the rubble of tired old caves to produce new goodies for biblical scholarship, why should we bury them again?

For today there are those who, ignoring the history of the KJV, feel God himself wrote every translated word as his special gift to the English world. Yeah, no kidding. It's unreal. Not that we're saying the KJV isn't a *good* translation, for it is. But we're here to suggest that later translations more accurately pinpoint the original Hebrew and Greek.

Howbeit, if thee prefer olde James, ye have thy preference, and needn't read on.

Version Explosion

Just as God sprinkled more and more bits of light about the life and coming of the Messiah as the Old Testament developed, he has seen fit in recent times to allow men to discover more information about his Word.

In the 1800s man's scholarship and research increased, better manuscripts containing Scripture were found, and archeologists dug up cities which only the Bible had claimed ever existed.

We've already mentioned how Cambridge and Blayney came up with their revisions of the KJV in 1762 and 1769—definite improvements, perhaps, but not officially backed by the government.

Protestant clergy and those academic types who flip pages with the end of their nose banded together in the mid-nineteenth century and determined the need for a new official version of the Bible.

In 1870 a Convocation of the Province of Canterbury was called for the purpose of revising the KJV where Hebrew and Greek texts had been carelessly translated. OK. We'll skip the day-by-day reports and how many bottles of ink they went through. Briefly, English and American scholars worked together and finally, on May 17, 1881, the *English Revised Version of the New Testament* was published.

Three days later the Revised Version (RV) appeared in the United States, and that week the entire New Testament was published in the *Chicago Tribune* and *Chicago Times.*

The RV's Old Testament was published in 1885. The RV's text, compared to the KJV, is much more accurate, more precise, more scholarly as to source material, better translated. So the people blew their minds and tossed the KJV away, right?

Wrong.

Christians who had grown up with the KJV somehow got the impression that this was it.

God's Word. Word for word. With no chance for error. Besides, they didn't like the way those "new" phrases and rhythmic patterns kept popping up all over the place.

The RV was not by any means the best translation which could have been produced, even though it was a major improvement over the KJV. In fact, the American committee which helped on the RV was still not satisfied with the final results, but promised to remain respectfully quiet for a period of fourteen years. Then, in 1901, the brash American scholars ended their silence.

The American Standard Edition of the Revised Version made the Bible scene. The editors of this American Standard Version (ASV) added page headings, juggled paragraph construction, and switched a few words around. As one example, the ASV reads "Holy Spirit" instead of the KJV and RV's "Holy Ghost." For many believers it's easier to think God as Spirit than perhaps as a white-sheeted monster named "Casper."

The ASV made headway in one American church after another, appealing to many American Christians more than the RV, and was then introduced to England.

Soon it was time for the RV to undergo a face lift.

In 1937 the International Council of Religious

Education authorized a committee to work on a new revision which would: ". . . embody the best results of modern scholarship as to the meaning of the Scriptures, and express this meaning in English diction which is designed for use in public and private worship and preserves those qualities which have given to the KJV a supreme place in English literature."

Dig? What they said was "hit it again, Sam." They simply wanted to make use of modern discoveries and linguistic skill to come up with an even juicier version. World War II slowed things up a bit, but *The Revised Standard Version: The New Testament* was published in 1946 with the Old Testament following in 1952.

When it comes to Bible translations you're never going to please all the people all of the time. Sometimes never. The ASV had been criticized for being too "literal" in the Old Testament, and now the Revised Standard Version (RSV) was under attack for watering down messianic passages.

In Isaiah 7:14 the Lord predicts the Messiah will be born of, in the Hebrew, an *almah*. This means a young maiden, or, more specifically, an unmarried female. The RSV reads "young woman" whereas other translations read "virgin." Conservative scholars agree that the fact Jesus was born of a virgin is critical to the faith, and the rendering of "young woman" could easily dilute the predicted miracle. Theology *is* involved in all translations.

Not exactly thrilled with the RSV, the General Assembly of the Church of Scotland met in 1946 in order to do their own thing with the Scriptures. The results, published in 1961, came out as the *New English Bible.* During the first year the British and Americans gobbled up four million copies.

At best, it's a distant cousin to the ASV and RSV since it often wanders away from more traditional interpretations of the original Greek. Some criticize its version of prophetic passages relating to the end of our age. *The New English Bible,* regardless of its shortcomings, is a competent translation.

Protestants were not the only ones concerned with new versions of the Bible. The Roman Catholics published the Rheims-Douay Bible (1582, 1609), the Challoner revision (1750), the Confraternity of Christian Doctrine edition which is used in America (1941), and a 1949 version by Monsignor Ronald A. Knox, used in England.

The Catholic translations were based on Jerome's Latin Vulgate—and thereby became English translations of a translation. The *Confraternity* edition uses more reliable Latin texts and even original texts for much of the Old Testament.

The "liberal" side of the body of Catholic biblical scholars came up with the Jerusalem Bible in the 1960s, an attempt to weed out the KJV style and use "modern" English.

Since 1853 British and American synagogues (or Jewish temples) had used Isaac Leeser's version of the Hebrew Bible. Then in 1892 the Jewish Publication Society of America decided to revise Leeser's work, but developed a new translation instead. The society's version of the Hebrew Bible in English was published in 1917 and is very similar to the ASV. In 1962 the society again modernized its translation and published *The Torah; A New Translation of the Holy Scriptures according to the Masoretic text*.

During the late 1800s several versions of the Bible were stacked on the shelves, each with a different approach or emphasis.

In 1902 a group of twenty pastors and laymen sought to present the Bible in modern American English. Not satisfied with short titles, the group called it *The Twentieth Century New Testament: A New Translation into Modern English Made from the Original Greek*.

OK. Hold up a minute. What's with this urge by Bible lovers to transform the Scripture into modern English? Did they do it for the bread? The glory? The kicks? Nope, they did it to make it easier to find out what God's trying to tell you *today*. And here are the most well-known efforts:

The Berkeley Version in Modern English (1945), Old Testament (1959). Gerrit Verkuyl of Berkeley, California, translated the New Testament and edited the Old Testament. He attempted to clear up any messianic prophecies which others had muddied and did not set God's words in quotes, considering the entire Bible as the Word of God. It's considered a good translation although perhaps its Old Testament is spotted with editorial mistakes.

J. B. Phillips wrote *Letters to Young Churches* (1947), *The Gospels in Modern English* (1952), *The Young Church in Action* (1955), *The Book of Revelation* (1957) and his one-volume finished work, *The New Testament in Modern English* (1958). Phillips often walks a tightrope between a translation and a paraphrase, a meaning-for-meaning treatment of the text. His books are very popular and offer a clear insight into the Scriptures.

The Authentic New Testament (1955) was written by Hugh J. Schonfield, a well-known Jewish scholar. He successfully brings to life the Jewish religious and social habits of the New Testament but—not having discovered that Jesus is his own promised Messiah—has missed out on the sensitivity only a believer can feel.

The Lockman Foundation published *The*

Amplified New Testament (1958), which attempts to greatly expand the Bible by offering a variety of meanings suggested by the text.

The Amplified Old Testament (1962, 1964) follows the same pattern and creates an atmosphere of a commentary as well as a translation.

The foundation gained respect and attention with the *Amplified*; both attributes increased in 1963 with the publication of *The New American Standard Bible, New Testament* and then the complete *New American Standard Bible,* containing both testaments, in 1971. *The New American Standard Bible* (NASB) is a revision of the already excellent American Standard Version of 1901. The NASB is a *translation,* not a paraphrase, and is extremely popular among those wishing to receive an easy-to-read, word-by-word English presentation of God's Word from the original Hebrew and Greek texts.

The American Bible Society called its 1966 publication *Good News for Modern Man*: *The New Testament in Today's English.* The good news is not only the gospel it presents but also the way in which *Good News for Modern Man* edits the Greek into a smooth-flowing pattern of thought.

Question time. Have you noticed the Scripture quoted in this book? Easy to understand, right? Almost as if someone were speaking directly to you. Not what you might think you would find in an old-fashioned, black-covered Bible with small type you have to squint at.

The particular Scripture quoted is from *The Living Bible,* published in 1971. *The Living Bible* is a paraphrase, not a direct translation, but it so captures the message of God through history that it's rapidly becoming one of the most demanded versions.

Kenneth N. Taylor, its translator, began doing his thing in 1962 when he published *Living Letters*: *The Paraphrased Epistles.* He followed this with *Living Prophecies* (1965), *Living Gospels* (1966), *Living Psalms and Proverbs* (1967), *Living Lessons of Life and Love* (1968), *Living Books of Moses* (1969), and *Living History of Israel* (1970)—all in the same style.

Of *Living Letters,* Taylor wrote: "This book is a paraphrase of the New Testament letters. Its purpose is to say as exactly as possible what Paul, James, Peter, John, and Jude meant, and to say it simply, expanding where necessary for a clear understanding by the modern reader."

Taylor admits it may swerve a little from a straight road of direct translation, but that's what a paraphrase is all about. The purpose is to communicate and be relevant, not confusing.

For those who have never plunged into what God has to say to man, but have listened instead to various fantasies from one weird dude after another, then . . .

Go ahead. Try a paraphrased version of the Bible. Like *The Living Bible* or *Good News for Modern Man.* Then if you feel ready to dig even deeper into the message of his Spirit, pick up a copy of, say, the *New American Standard,* a translation, and read on.

Many theologians as well as good old solid believers use a paraphrase and a translation together. One helps the other.

OK, team, one last chapter comin' up. Our last chance to hook you on the only true revolutionary—the mild-mannered carpenter, who loves and understands you better than *anyone.*

So flip the page. The best is yet to come!

So What?

Do you feel as if you had shot the rapids on a raft, while trying to search the shoreline for signs giving a historical background of the English Bible?

We hope that you have picked up bits and pieces of new information without feeling drowned in a thousand text books written in Oldde Englysshe.

So what? That is, what's the point of exposing you to a book which you've thought was only carried on sunny Sunday mornings by little old ladies wearing purple hats and tennis shoes? If you've remembered anything at all from this Book, we hope you remember this . . .

We claim that not only is God alive, but that he's written a book to get man's head together and let him know how he stands in relation to both God and other human beings. This book, with an Old and New Testament, contains wisdom, love, philosophy, psychology, history, and understanding far beyond what any group of Ph.D.s could gather up.

Most people couldn't care less about God or the book. But God, because he's alive and well and living everywhere, does care about people.

Through the centuries this Book has been maintained by its Writer, if not by earth's inhabitants. Man's own ego trips have often blinded him to the light of God's truth, but that doesn't mean the light was hiding in a dark corner.

Say, do you ever get the feeling there really isn't any purpose in life except to be born, live, and die? That maybe the sum total of your existence is to spend seventy years looking for something to do tomorrow? Then when tomorrow becomes today you complain about what a bummer yesterday was. And on and on and on.

Yet with all the war, poverty, sickness, and greed we have on earth there remains hope that tomorrow, *some* tomorrow, man will suddenly wake up and say, "Man, let's love one another *now* before we completely wipe ourselves out!"

You tell us. Where are you going to find this love for everyone? It seems mankind is talking about gold-plating a garbage dump. Pouring precious metal over a smelly heap of man's innate selfishness in order to keep the stench away from all us nice folks.

We can only suggest you give God a chance to help you put this whole bag into perspective.

Curious about how the world began and what happened after man blew his whole scene in the first garden by rebelling against his Creator? Read about it in Genesis.

Interested in the 613 laws of worship and daily living detailed to the Jewish nation—any one of which, not followed, would label a Jew as a transgressor with God? Read about it in Leviticus and Deuteronomy.

Curious how God promised to permanently bridge man's rebellion by offering the Messiah as the only acceptable sacrifice? Read the Psalms, Jeremiah, and Isaiah.

Ever hear that this Jesus of Nazareth claimed to be God's Son, the Messiah, and that he came to fulfill the Jewish laws and the prophets' predictions? Read Matthew. And Mark. And Luke. And John.

Wonder why this is relevant for you today? It's because this Jesus made a promise a long time ago that never ran out. He said: "Look! I have been standing at the door and I am constantly knocking. If anyone hears me calling him and opens the door, I will come in and fellowship with him and he with me" (Revelation 3:20).

What does it mean to have fellowship with him? It means a new life, a new perspective, a new hope. Where can you find out more about this life? Very simple.

The Bible.

"I have been crucified with Christ," Paul wrote, "and I myself no longer live, but Christ lives in me. And the real life I now have within this body is a result of my trusting in the Son of God, who loved me and gave himself for me" (Galatians 2:20).

It's as if you shed your old skin and put on a new one. As if you became, literally, a new person. And the person is Christ.

"For if you tell others with your own mouth that Jesus Christ is your Lord, and believe in your own heart that God has raised him from the dead, you will be saved" (Romans 10:9).

Hold it! Don't go away mad because a word was used which you associate with barefoot street preachers carrying signs which read: The World Ended Yesterday—Be (here it comes) Saved.

Saved merely refers to salvation. A drowning

man wants to be saved, not rehabilitated. Not improved. Salvation merely refers to what happens when a person simply believes that God's grace is his for the asking, but by faith in Jesus he receives an entrance into an eternal paradise that will be heavier than anything he could imagine. But don't take our word for it.

Read the Bible.

It also means God's Spirit comes to dwell within you. Jesus laid this on his followers when he explained how he would go back to heaven, then he'd send a "comforter," his Spirit. It would go like this: "When the Holy Spirit, who is truth, comes, he shall guide you into all truth, for he will not be presenting his own ideas, but will be passing on to you what he has heard" (John 16:13).

What about all you dudes who have believed in Jesus? What about you guys who have trusted in him, yet live your lives scared to death about what may or may not happen next week? Maybe you haven't been reading the Bible carefully enough. If you had, you might have come across something like: "And it is he who will supply all your needs from his riches in glory, because of what Christ Jesus has done for us" (Philippians 4:19).

Riches? When you don't have dime number one to buy what you need? Maybe you aren't praying to you-know-who, friend.

Maybe you aren't reading the Bible at all!

Listen, you should understand by now what God went through to preserve his Word over the centuries. You think he did this for laughs? C'mon, man. He did it because he loves you. Because he wants you to have an abundant life *now*. He wants to supply all your needs *now*. He wants to bring you closer to himself *now*.

You shouldn't have to wait until you meet him face to face before you groove on the goodies. He'd like to lay it on you now. After all, he made thousands of promises that he would. They're right there in black and white. In the Bible.

The Bible. He took all that time to get it into English—and you use it as a fancy paperweight.

The Bible. The Living Word of the one who made you—and you keep it on your shelf wedged between a book on astrology and an empty peanut butter jar.

The Bible. It accurately portrays the immediate, future history of mankind—and you sit there listening to mumbled predictions by Guru Goonschlock.

The Bible. A popular little book which lets you know everything you ever wanted to know about yourself. And about God.

If you're interested . . .